CODE RED
APRIL 16, 1947
The Texas City Disaster

by Linda Scher

Consultant: Archie P. McDonald
Director, East Texas Historical Association

BEARPORT
PUBLISHING

New York, New York

Credits

Cover and Title Page, © AP Images/U.S. Coast Guard; 4, © AP Images; 5, © Tim Wimborne/ Reuters; 7, © Moore Memorial Public Library; 8-9, © AP Images; 11, © M. Dillon/CORBIS; 12, © Moore Memorial Public Library; 13, © Bettmann/CORBIS; 14, © AP Images; 15, © AP Images; 16, © Houston Metropolitan Research Center, Houston Public Library, Texas; 17, © Keystone/Hulton Archive/Getty Images/Newscom.com; 18, © AP Images; 19, © Mark Pandanell; 20, © AP Images; 21, © Galveston Texas History Center/Rosenberg Library; 22, © AP Images/Handout via Texas City Sun; 23, © Galveston Texas History Center/ Rosenberg Library; 24, © Courtesy Library of Congress Prints and Photographs Division; 25, © Bettmann/CORBIS; 26, © Mark Pandanell; 27, © Mark Pandanell; 28T, © Mark Pandanell/Henry J. Baumgartner/Firepro911; 28B, © Houston Metropolitan Research Center, Houston Public Library, Texas; 29T, © Bettmann/CORBIS; 29B, © Bettmann/CORBIS.

Publisher: Kenn Goin
Project Editor: Adam Siegel
Creative Director: Spencer Brinker
Photo Researcher: Beaura Kathy Ringrose
Design: Dawn Beard Creative

Library of Congress Cataloging-in-Publication Data

Scher, Linda.
   The Texas City disaster / by Linda Scher.
      p. cm. — (Code red)
   Includes bibliographical references and index.
   Audience: Grades 4-6.
   ISBN-13: 978-1-59716-363-7 (library binding)
   ISBN-10: 1-59716-363-5 (library binding)
   1. Texas City (Tex.)—History—20th century—Juvenile literature. 2. Disasters— Texas—Texas City—History—20th century—Juvenile literature. 3. Fires—Texas— Texas City—History—20th century—Juvenile literature. 4. Explosions—Texas—Texas City—History—20th century—Juvenile literature. 5. Grandcamp (Ship)—Explosion, 1947—Juvenile literature. 6. High Flyer (Ship)—Explosion, 1947—Juvenile literature. 7. Texas City (Tex.)—Biography—Juvenile literature. I. Title.

   F394.T4S34 2007
   976.4'139063—dc22
                        2006029664

For more information, write to Bearport Publishing Company, Inc., 101 Fifth Avenue, Suite 6R, New York, New York 10003. Printed in the United States of America.

10 9 8 7 6 5 4 3 2 1

Contents

Loading the *Grandcamp*

It was 8:00 A.M. on April 16, 1947. **Dockworker** Julio Luna was loading heavy bags into the French ship *Grandcamp* in Texas City, Texas. The paper bags held **fertilizer** bound for farmers in Europe.

The fertilizer seemed harmless. It was just something farmers added to soil to help plants grow. However, it was made of **ammonium nitrate**. This chemical is also used to make bombs. When it gets very hot, it can explode. No one on the ship knew how dangerous the fertilizer could be.

Today, warning labels are placed on bags of ammonium nitrate.

The *Grandcamp* was 437 feet (133 m) long. It was almost 80 feet (24 m) longer than a football field.

Dangerous Cargo

As men dropped the paper bags filled with fertilizer into the *Grandcamp*'s **hold**, some ripped. They were still hot after arriving from the factory. Bits of warm paper and loose fertilizer may have mixed with other **cargo**. The ship now held the perfect **fuel** for a fire.

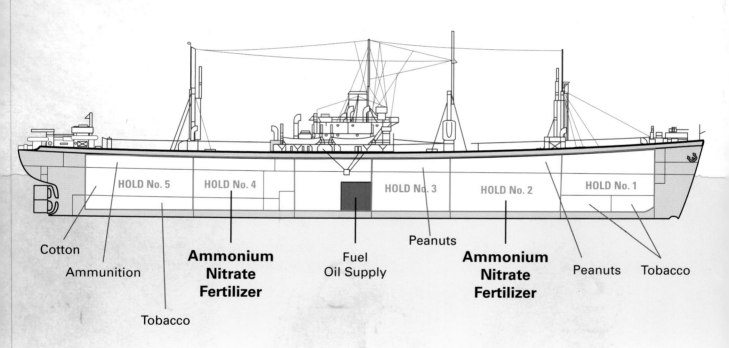

Cotton

Ammunition

Tobacco

Ammonium Nitrate Fertilizer

Fuel Oil Supply

Peanuts

Ammonium Nitrate Fertilizer

Peanuts

Tobacco

HOLD No. 5 · HOLD No. 4 · HOLD No. 3 · HOLD No. 2 · HOLD No. 1

This diagram shows where cargo was stored in the *Grandcamp*'s hold.

Along with fertilizer, the *Grandcamp*'s cargo included cotton, peanuts, and tobacco.

Blue smoke began to rise from the large pile of bags. "I smell paper burning!" Luna yelled. Deep in the ship's hold, a fire had begun.

Dockworkers rushed to pour water on the flames, but the fire still spread. The ship's captain feared more water would ruin his cargo. So he ordered his crew to pump steam into the hold instead. The French captain's decision would soon have deadly results.

The Texas City dock area, before the fire

A Growing Fire

Workers sent clouds of hot steam into the *Grandcamp*'s hold. The captain hoped the steam would smother the fire. Yet the flames kept growing.

Peter Suderman, the dockworkers' **supervisor**, ran to call the fire department. Within minutes, four fire trucks raced to the dock, sirens screaming.

Members of the Texas City Volunteer Fire Department worked to control the blaze.

By 9:00 A.M., flames were shooting out of the ship's **hatch**. A crowd of curious people had gathered at the waterfront to watch. They did not know, however, that they were in terrible danger. Soon, the fire would turn into one of the worst disasters in U.S. history.

> "This is a dangerous fire, and we need all the help we can get."
>
> —Fire Chief Henry Baumgartner, telling a coworker to call city hall

There were about 2,300 tons (2,086 metric tons) of fertilizer aboard the *Grandcamp*.

Texas City, Texas

In 1947, Texas City was a busy **port** on the Gulf of Mexico. The *Grandcamp* and its crew had come there from France. Many ships came to Texas City from other countries. These ships carried cargo such as oil and gasoline to places all over the world.

Texas City is located near the southeastern corner of the state of Texas.

In 1946, more than 13,441,000 tons (12,193,470 metric tons) of cargo traveled through the port of Texas City.

Texas City had four oil **refineries**. They turned the oil into gasoline before it was shipped. The town also had two large chemical companies. These businesses stored huge tanks of **flammable** chemicals and oil near the dock. On that spring day in 1947, they were dangerously close to the blazing *Grandcamp*.

"We weren't prepared for disaster."
—Ken LeMaet, a business leader in Texas City

Today, there are still oil refineries in Texas City.

The First Blast

When Texas City's firefighters arrived at the dock, they rushed to the *Grandcamp*. They unwound their hoses and began spraying the ship. However, it had become so hot that the water quickly turned to steam.

As the firefighters battled the blaze, the ship began to creak and shake. Enormous pressure was building up in the steamy hold.

Black smoke from the *Grandcamp* rose 2,000 feet (610 m) into the air. It was shaped like a huge mushroom.

Suddenly, the hatch covering the hold burst open. Huge flames leaped out. A thick cloud of orange smoke covered the **deck**. Then, at 9:12 A.M., the ammonium nitrate in the *Grandcamp* exploded. The ship was ripped apart. All the firefighters were killed. Nothing was left of the city's four fire trucks but twisted metal.

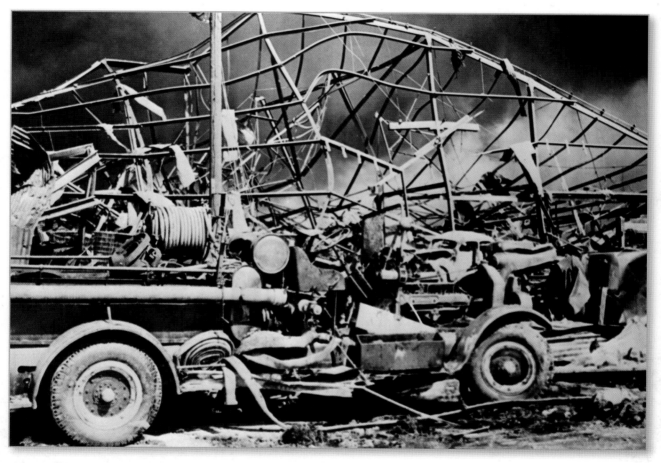

The explosion destroyed this Texas City fire truck.

66 Send the Red Cross! There's been a big explosion and thousands are injured! 99

—John Urquhart, Southwestern Bell Telephone Company supervisor, calling the city of Houston for help

No Warning, No Escape

The explosion happened so quickly that no one on board had time to escape. The captain, crew, and dockworkers on the ship all died instantly.

Debris from the blast flew toward people on the dock. A deadly rain of red-hot metal, burning rope, and knife-sharp glass covered the crowd.

Fireballs of burning metal smashed windows and set roofs on fire. The nearby Monsanto chemical plant went up in flames. Giant tanks filled with highly flammable fuel were set **ablaze**. Parents ran coughing and screaming from their homes, carrying terrified children.

The blast from the *Grandcamp* set the Monsanto chemical plant on fire. More than a hundred workers were killed.

The U.S. Coast Guard used boats to help put out the fire at the chemical plant.

The blast was so powerful that it flung the *Grandcamp*'s 1.5-ton (1.36-metric ton) anchor 2 miles (3 km) away. It was stuck in the ground 10 feet (3 m) deep.

15

Shock Wave and Tidal Wave

The huge explosion sent a powerful blast of air hurtling through the sky. This **shock wave** smashed into two small airplanes flying over the port. Both planes crashed into the water. Everyone on board was killed.

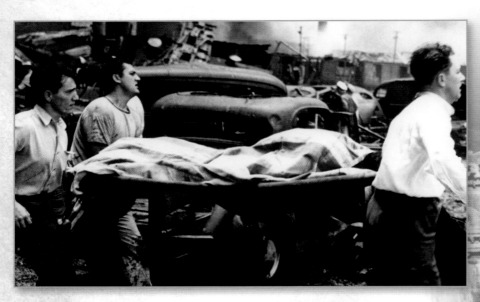

Volunteers carried the dead and injured away from the dock area.

The *Grandcamp* explosion broke windows as far away as 10 miles (16 km).

The explosion also created a gigantic **tidal wave**. The 15-foot-high (4.5-m) wave crashed onto the dock, covering the crowd. Some people drowned instantly. The deadly wave dragged others out to sea.

The tidal wave washed ashore the 150-foot (46-m) steel barge *Longhorn II*, which weighed 30 tons (27 metric tons).

A Second Blast

By late afternoon, it seemed the worst was over. Then someone reported smoke coming from another cargo ship, the *High Flyer*.

Late that night, workers learned that the *High Flyer* was also carrying ammonium nitrate. It could explode, like the *Grandcamp*! **Tugboats** had to get the ship away from the dock quickly.

After the *Grandcamp* exploded, U.S. troops formed a roadblock to stop people from entering Texas City.

The tugboats moved the *High Flyer* about 100 feet (30 m). Then flames started shooting out of its hold. The tugboats sped away minutes before the *High Flyer* blew up. It was 1:10 A.M. on April 17. Only 16 hours had passed since Texas City's first disaster.

The *High Flyer*'s propeller can be seen today in Texas City.

" Three minutes after we left, a tremendous blast blew the *High Flyer* apart. I saw steel bigger than cars flying through the air. **"**

–J. D. Babin, a crew member on a tugboat sent to tow the *High Flyer*

When the *High Flyer* exploded, thousands of tiny pieces of the ship flew like missiles through the air. Some landed more than a mile (1.6 km) away.

To the Rescue

As news of the blasts spread, help poured in from near and far. People who lived in Texas City helped frightened children find their parents. They rescued people trapped in damaged buildings.

At the bus station and airport, Boy Scouts greeted relief workers from out of town. The Scouts took them wherever help was most needed.

Rescue workers searched through debris in the hopes of finding survivors.

Medical teams and firefighters rushed to Texas City from Galveston and other nearby towns. Soon 12 fire departments were battling the blazes.

About 2,000 doctors and nurses came, too. Right away, they started setting up hospitals and first-aid stations for the injured.

" Patients were arriving at the clinic mostly on foot and were everywhere in the clinic they could sit, lean, or lie. "

—Bertha Anderson, a nurse who helped treat the wounded

The Red Cross sent much needed supplies, such as medicine, clean water, and blankets.

About 10,000 blankets and 2,600 cots were sent to Texas City to help the victims.

A High Toll

The Texas City disaster was the worst **industrial** accident in U.S. history. When it was over, more than 550 people were dead. The city had lost 28 brave firefighters. At least 3,500 people were injured. Many, such as Mary Hunter, had serious cuts and burns.

After the disaster, more than a third of the 1,500 houses in Texas City were damaged or destroyed. About 2,000 people were left homeless.

Mary Hunter had worked at the Monsanto chemical plant. She was chatting with a friend when the *Grandcamp* exploded. Flying glass sliced through her right arm.

Over the next six years, doctors operated many times to remove the pieces of glass. Mary spent weeks recovering from each of the painful surgeries. She was never fully able to use her right arm again.

People fled from Texas City to Galveston, Houston, and other towns in Texas.

66 I was grief-stricken, but not nearly as much as my mother. I don't think she ever really got over it. 99

—Forrest Walker, a high school student whose father died in the disaster

Seeking Justice

Many people in Texas City blamed the U.S. government for the disaster. If officials had told them the fertilizer was dangerous, the tragedy might never have happened. The people of Texas City took the government to court.

In 1950, they won their case. Judges ruled that government officials should have explained how to handle ammonium nitrate safely.

Texas senator Lyndon B. Johnson wanted Congress to pass a law helping Texas City.

"What the government should have done, and it was so simple, was just put warnings on the bags. They just didn't warn people."

—Henry Dalehite, Jr., Texas City lawyer and judge

Government lawyers, however, disagreed. In 1953, judges on the U.S. **Supreme Court** looked at the case again. They decided the government had done nothing wrong.

Still, some people felt the government should help the survivors of the disaster. So in 1955, Congress passed a special act that gave Texas City **citizens** about $16.5 million.

With a close 4–3 vote, the judges on the Supreme Court decided the government was not to blame for the Texas City disaster.

More than 3,000 lawsuits were filed against the U.S. government as a result of the Texas City disaster.

Learning from Texas City

After the Texas City disaster, people looked for ways to prevent similar accidents. The U.S. government made new rules for packing, loading, and shipping dangerous chemicals. Things made with ammonium nitrate had to have special warning labels. Some cities stopped ships carrying ammonium nitrate from entering their ports.

The *Grandcamp*'s anchor can be seen today in Texas City.

In 1998, the government created the U.S. Chemical Safety Board. The board looks into the causes of chemical accidents in the past to help prevent future disasters.

Cities across the country made disaster plans in case an emergency happened. Where would people go if they were hurt? Where could they stay until the danger was over? How would they get food and water?

Nothing could change what happened in Texas City. Yet the new rules and plans would help keep other cities safe in the future.

This fountain and statue in Texas City were built to remember the firefighters who lost their lives during the disaster.

Profiles

Many people played an important role in the events connected to the Texas City disaster. Here are three of them.

Henry Baumgartner was the chief of the Texas City Volunteer Fire Department for 20 years.

- Had another full-time job buying supplies for the Texas City Terminal Railway
- Was well liked by local citizens
- Was standing on the deck of the ship directing the firefighting effort when the *Grandcamp* exploded

Curtis Trahan was the mayor of Texas City at the time of the disaster.

- Was a World War II (1939–1945) veteran
- During the crisis, showed strong leadership and worked hard to keep citizens calm
- After the disaster, had first-aid stations set up and helped organize disaster relief efforts
- Asked for help from the Texas State Guard, U.S. Coast Guard, and other government agencies

Lyndon Baines Johnson represented Texas in the U.S. Senate from 1948 to 1960.

- Became Senate majority leader in 1955
- Helped convince Congress to pass a law giving money to some Texas City disaster victims
- Served as the 36th president of the United States from 1963 to 1969

Glossary

ablaze (uh-BLAZE) on fire

ammonium nitrate
(uh-MOH-nee-uhm NYE-trate)
a chemical compound used in
making explosives and fertilizer

cargo (KAR-goh) goods carried
by ship, airplane, or truck

citizens (SIT-i-zuhnz) people who
live in a particular country, city,
or town

debris (duh-BREE)
scattered pieces of something
that has been destroyed

deck (DEK) a floor that extends
from one side of a ship to the
other

dockworker (DOK-*wur*-kur)
a person who loads and unloads
cargo from a ship

fertilizer (FUR-tuh-*lize*-ur)
a substance added to soil to make
plants grow better

flammable (FLAM-uh-buhl)
something that can be set on fire
easily and burns quickly

fuel (FYOO-uhl) something that
is used as a source of energy or
heat, such as gasoline

hatch (HACH) the cover for an
opening on the deck of a ship

hold (HOHLD) the place below a
ship's deck where cargo is stored

industrial (in-DUHSS-tree-uhl)
having to do with factories or
businesses

port (PORT) a place where boats
stay to load or unload cargo

refineries (ri-FYE-nuh-reez)
plants or factories that make oil,
metals, or sugar into a usable
product that can be sold to
customers

shock wave (SHOK WAYV)
an air wave, produced by an
explosion, that moves with great
force and at a high speed

supervisor (SOO-pur-*vye*-zur)
a person who is in charge of
other workers

Supreme Court
(suh-PREEM KORT)
the highest court in the U.S.
legal system, consisting of nine
judges or justices

tidal wave (TIDE-uhl WAYV)
a large and powerful ocean
wave caused by an earthquake,
landslide, or explosion

tugboats (TUHG-bohts)
powerful boats used to tow or
push other ships

Bibliography

Minutaglio, Bill. *City on Fire: The Forgotten Disaster That Devastated a Town and Ignited a Landmark Legal Battle.* New York: HarperCollins (2003).

Stephens, Hugh W. *The Texas City Disaster, 1947.* Austin, TX: University of Texas Press (1997).

The Handbook of Texas Online. "Texas City Disaster." (**www.tsha.utexas.edu/handbook/online/articles/TT/lyt1.html**)

Texas City, Texas, Disaster: April 16, 17, 1947. Report by The Fire Prevention and Engineering Bureau of Texas and The National Board of Fire Underwriters. (**www.local1259iaff.org/report.htm**)

Read More

Landau, Elaine. *Fires.* New York: Franklin Watts (1999).

Raatma, Lucia. *Fire Safety.* Chanhassen, MN: Child's World (2004).

Woods, Michael, and Mary B. Woods. *Fires (Disasters Up Close).* Minneapolis, MN: Lerner Publishing (2007).

Learn More Online

To learn more about the Texas City disaster, fire safety, and firefighting, visit **www.bearportpublishing.com/CodeRed**

Index

About the Author

Linda Scher has written several fiction and nonfiction books.
She also writes for *Kids Discover*, a magazine for young people.
She has a nephew who is a full-time firefighter
with the fire department in Raleigh, North Carolina.